OUR WORLD IN CRISIS

POVERTY

RACHEL MINAY

FRANKLIN WATTS
LONDON•SYDNEY

Franklin Watts
First published in Great Britain in 2018 by The Watts Publishing Group
Copyright © The Watts Publishing Group, 2018

Produced for Franklin Watts by
White-Thomson Publishing Ltd
www.wtpub.co.uk

ISBN: 978 1 4451 6381 9

Credits
Series Editor: Izzi Howell
Series Designer: Dan Prescott, Couper Street Type Co.
Series Consultant: Philip Parker

The publisher would like to thank the following for permission to reproduce their pictures: Alamy: Jake Lyell/CARE 16, jean-marc Teychenne 18, GeoPic 35, ACORN 6 44; Getty: Leon Neal 7, HUGO PHILPOT/AFP 13t, Aldo Pavan 15, Bernard Bisson/Sygma 17b, Eivaisla 24, ALBERT GONZALEZ FARRAN/AFP 25t, NurPhoto 28, Godong/UIG 41b; Shutterstock: Thomas Amler cover, Stephane Bidouze title page and 33, R.M. Nunes 4, Fitria Ramli 6t, Iakov Filimonov 6b, robertonencini 10, thomas koch 11, Philip Mowbray 13b, franshendrik Tambunan 14, Joseph Sohm 17t, Anton_ Ivanov 19, Baiterek Media 21, Slava Samusevich 22, StanislavBeloglazov 23, Suzanne Tucker 25b, bodom 26, Keep Smiling Photography 27t, chingyunsong 27b, JHVEPhoto 29, gary yim 30t, John Wollwerth 32t, LP2 Studio 37, Tukaram.Karve 39t&c, Avatar_023 39b, Stefano Ember 40, lev radin 41t, Thinglass 43, Ehab Othman 45; UNDP Brazil: 36; United Nations: 38; WaterAid: Tom Greenwood 31, Sibtain Haider 42, Anna Kari 30b, James Kiyimba 32b; Wikimedia: 8.

All design elements from Shutterstock.

Please note:
The website addresses (URLs) included in this book were valid at the time of going to press. However, because of the nature of the Internet, it is possible that some addresses may have changed, or sites may have changed or closed down since publication. While the author and publishers regret any inconvenience this may cause to the readers, no responsibility for any such changes can be accepted by either the author or the publishers.

Printed in Malaysia

Franklin Watts
An imprint of
Hachette Children's Group
Part of The Watts Publishing Group
Carmelite House
50 Victoria Embankment
London EC4Y 0DZ

An Hachette UK Company
www.hachette.co.uk
www.franklinwatts.co.uk

CONTENTS

What is POVERTY?

We all know that some people are richer than us and others are poorer; we may think of the area we live in as being more or less well off than other neighbourhoods. But what is poverty? Is it to do with what we have compared with others around us, or is it to do with what we need to survive?

Rich and poor

What do you think of when you hear the words 'rich' and 'poor'? Perhaps you think that being 'rich' means having a big house, more than one car and taking lots of holidays. Possibly you think that someone who is rich has more than they need. Does being 'poor' mean not having some of these things, or is it more extreme than that – for example having so little food that you get sick easily or are hungry or starving?

This family lives in rural India. The children are not wearing shoes, but they are well clothed and also wearing necklaces and bracelets. Their home may look very different to yours, but does this mean they are poor?

No choice

Poverty can mean different things to different people. However, it always means having no choice in life and little opportunity to change things.

Extreme poverty

A simple way to think of the different levels of poverty is in terms of 'wants' and 'needs'. Extreme poverty or absolute poverty is when people lack the basic things they need to live.

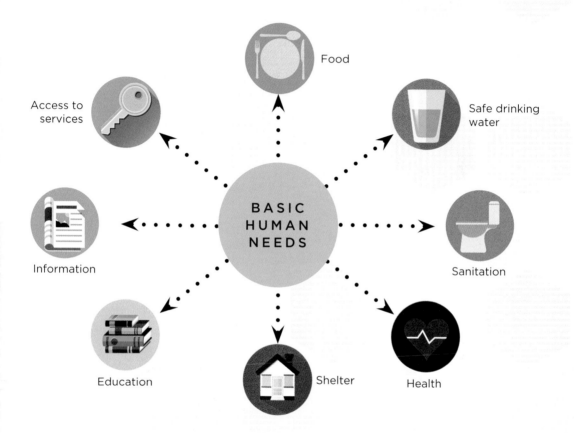

Food

Access to services

Safe drinking water

BASIC HUMAN NEEDS

Information

Sanitation

Education

Shelter

Health

The good news is that in recent years the number of people living in extreme poverty has been declining. However, there is much more to be done. In 2015, 836 million people were still living in extreme poverty – that is over 11 per cent of the world population.

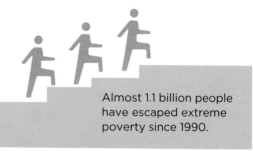

EXTREME POVERTY IS DECLINING

Almost 1.1 billion people have escaped extreme poverty since 1990.

Measuring poverty

Poverty is usually measured using people's incomes. The most widely used measure is the international poverty line, which is decided by the World Bank. Since 2015, the line has been set at US $1.90 – this means that people who have less than US $1.90 a day to live on are considered to be living in extreme poverty.

The international poverty line can be used to compare poverty between countries. Another way is to look at something called purchasing power (how much can be bought with one unit of currency in the country).

These skyscrapers are a sign of the wealth in Doha, the capital city and economic centre of Qatar. In terms of actual purchasing power, Qatar is the richest country in the world.

Relative poverty

Relative poverty is when people are poor compared to others living in the same country. This might mean a family not being able to afford a car or TV when most people around them can. In another country, it might mean not having decent housing or being able to buy new shoes. In still others, it might mean not having clean water, getting enough nourishing food or being able to afford an education.

In more developed regions, such as Australia, North America and many countries in Europe, some people may feel poor if they cannot afford gadgets such as expensive mobile phones.

Poor in a rich country

When thinking about poverty, it's important to remember that this isn't just something that affects people in what are sometimes called 'developing countries'. Poverty is also a serious issue for many people living in what we think of as the developed or industrialised world.

Children growing up in poverty in the developed world are disadvantaged in ways that affect their future lives. For example, in 2013/14, 60.5 per cent of children in the UK received at least five GCSEs; for disadvantaged children eligible for free school meals, the number shrank to just 33.5 per cent.

CASE STUDY

Food-bank use in the UK

Poverty is a growing problem in the UK. In 2017, it was reported that food-bank use in the UK had reached a record high – with 1.2 million food parcels having been given to people in need in the preceding year. What's more, this was the ninth year in a row that demand at food banks had gone up.

People turn to food banks like this for a variety of reasons. These might include changes in or delays to benefits, or sudden bills for people on a low income.

What can you do?

Donate to a food bank. Many supermarkets have a collection point near the tills or you can donate to a food bank directly. You can find a list of suitable items to include at www.trusselltrust.org/get-help/emergency-food/food-parcel/.

Why are PEOPLE POOR?

In many ways the world is rich, yet around one in every ten people is extremely poor. Some of the causes of poverty are rooted in the past, while others are linked to the present.

What is inequality?

'Inequality' means 'not being equal' and it is usually used to describe the unfair way that some people have more money or opportunities than others. Poverty and inequality are very closely linked, and many people believe that a country getting richer is not enough on its own to reduce poverty – inequality must be reduced as well.

Is the world rich or poor?

Overall, the world has been steadily growing richer: this is despite periods of global economic crisis, such as the Great Depression of the 1930s and the financial crisis of 2007–08.

However, the way the world's wealth is shared out is extremely unequal. Over time, inequality builds up and the gap widens – another way of saying this is 'the rich get richer and the poor get poorer'.

The Great Depression started in the USA, but spread around the world. This photo from 1931 shows unemployed men queuing for food at a soup kitchen.

 **71 per cent** of adults own less than US $10,000 in wealth (money and goods) – this represents just **3 per cent** of the world's wealth.

 The world's wealthiest people (those who own over US $100,000) represent just **8.1 per cent** of the adult population but hold **84.6 per cent** of the world's wealth.

 Just **eight** men own the same as the combined wealth of the **3.6 billion** people who make up the poorest half of the world.

Colonialism

One of the causes of this inequality has its roots in the past. Many of the world's richer countries have become wealthy at the expense of countries that are now among the world's poorest.

During the nineteenth century, many powerful countries in Europe such as Britain, the Netherlands, France, Spain and Portugal colonised (took control of) other parts of the world, particularly in Africa, South America and the Caribbean. They used the colonies' natural resources, manufactured them into goods in Europe and then sold them at a much higher price, often to the countries where the resources had come from. In this way, the colonial powers got richer over time.

Although the colonies gained independence in the second half of the twentieth century, the years of inequality meant that many were already at a disadvantage. Also, these countries often suffered major problems such as wars and debt, combined with poor governance, poor infrastructure and reduced opportunities for education. This resulted in a situation that made it desperately hard to escape poverty.

War and conflict

Poverty and conflict are closely linked, although it can be hard to know if poverty causes conflict or conflict causes poverty.

Does poverty cause conflict?

Poverty means desperate people are in fierce competition for few resources and a growing gap between rich and poor can make people angry. Civil wars (wars fought between different groups of people within the same country or state) are most common in poor countries. Poverty can also destroy the links that keep a society together, such as people feeling safe and having the opportunity to make a life for themselves and their families. This also makes conflict more likely.

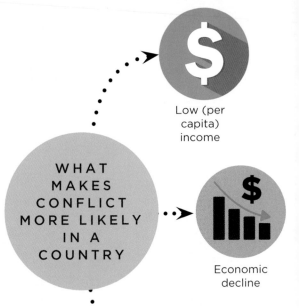

Low (per capita) income

WHAT MAKES CONFLICT MORE LIKELY IN A COUNTRY

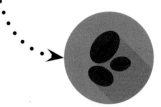

Economic decline

Dependence on primary commodities, such as coffee or rice (see page 14)

Sierra Leone is slowly recovering from a brutal civil war (1991–2002) and an outbreak of the deadly Ebola epidemic in 2014. Poverty is still a barrier to girls' education in the country – nearly half of girls and young women aged 15–24 cannot read or write.

Does conflict cause poverty?

Conflict takes money away from services and development and leads to the loss of livelihoods, which increases poverty. There are a number of economic costs to a war, including loss of production and the expense of repairing roads or buildings that have been damaged by bombs. More money being spent on the military is likely to take money away from other services, such as health or education.

Refugees and IDPs

In times of conflict, it is also likely that wealth – both in terms of money and people – moves out of the country, which also breaks down families and communities. Refugees are people who are forced to leave their country because of war, persecution or violence. Internally displaced persons (IDPs) are people who are forced to leave their homes for the same reasons, but who stay in the same country.

Armed conflict affects all aspects of everyday life and can make people desperate and angry. Millions of ordinary Syrians have been forced to leave their homes and jobs since the war began.

CASE STUDY

Syria – the refugee crisis

Civil war began in Syria in 2011. Since that time, more than 4.9 million people have fled Syria and a further six million are displaced within the country. Many of these people live in poverty: families cannot afford to feed their children and children cannot continue their education.

Debt

One of the biggest problems for poor countries is debt, which is also linked to the history of colonialism.

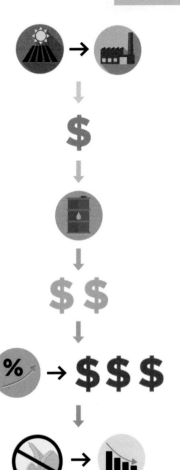

When the former colonies gained their independence, they changed their economies from being based on farming to manufacturing, which required investment.

They borrowed money from richer countries. Some people think the banks lent money irresponsibly. Another problem was corruption, which meant that not all of the loan money even went to the purpose it was intended for.

An oil crisis in 1973 hit the countries hard. Countries that are trying to industrialise need to import more oil, but also the crisis meant oil prices went up.

Countries borrowed more money to continue importing oil.

Interest rates went up, meaning the countries now owed more and more in debt interest payments.

The economic growth that people had hoped for didn't happen, especially in sub-Saharan Africa. Poor harvests and lower crop prices, together with rising oil prices, led to falling economic growth and so less money from taxes.

When countries struggle to repay these huge debts, they often cut services that are most important to the poorest people, such as health and education.

Drop the debt?

Towards the end of the 1990s, many people started to campaign for governments to cancel the old debts that poor countries owed. Cancelling debt is not a simple issue, because it could mean richer countries decide to stop lending or cut the amount of money they give in aid (see page 40). However, campaigners said that the total amount of the debt was not that significant in terms of the income of the developed world. They also argued that if the debts were written off once, the poorer countries could start afresh and put the money they were spending on interest payments into important local development and services.

In 1996, the HIPC (Heavily Indebted Poor Countries) Initiative was launched, which aimed to address some of these issues by reducing debts to levels that governments can manage without having to cut back on investment in reducing poverty. By 2017, the HIPC Initiative had approved debt-reduction packages for 36 countries, representing US $76 billion in debt-service relief over time.

Personal debt

Debt is not just a country-level problem. Personal debt can be devastating for the poor all around the world. People who have borrowed even a small amount of money, but then find they are unable to pay it back – perhaps because crops fail or ill health means they are unable to work – can then find themselves in a devastating spiral of debt.

The Jubilee 2000 campaign called for the debts of developing countries to be cancelled.

In 2017, a survey run by a UK debt charity found that some people were forced to go without food or basic furniture because they had run up debts on rent or utility bills.

Trade and globalisation

In the past, most people grew or caught their own food, built their own homes and made the things they needed. This is called being self-sufficient. Now, most people are linked into the global world of buying and selling. Some people think globalisation (the way the world is becoming increasingly connected through trade and communication) is the answer to poverty. However, others argue that competition on the worldwide stage is not fair. Richer, more developed countries have advantages such as bigger markets and better technology. They are also able to support their own industries through subsidies (money paid to industries to compensate for keeping prices low and therefore competitive).

Countries that open up to trade can experience rapid economic growth. Indonesia, the largest economy in Southeast Asia, has reduced its poverty rate by half since 1999 to 10.9 per cent in 2016.

Overdependence

Poor countries often trade in primary commodities – these are 'raw' materials, such as coffee, tea, sugar or rice. Many are heavily dependent on these commodities, so are seriously affected when prices for that commodity fall. This uncertainty can then make it hard for these countries to plan development. One possible solution to this is growing higher-priced commodities. Another is moving away from growing to manufacturing goods for export, although this involves huge initial investment.

Fair trade

World trade is often very unfair – particularly for the farmers at the beginning of the chain. Fair trade aims to help the producers in developing countries get paid a fair price for their commodities and promotes sustainable farming. Buying things that have been certified as fair trade means that you are helping to support these farmers and their families.

Fair-trade things that you can buy include foodstuffs such as tea and chocolate, flowers and clothes made from fair-trade cotton. Fair-trade products are often (but not always) a bit more expensive than alternatives, but this is because producers are being paid a decent living wage – not a really low wage.

Flowers are a higher-value product than many primary commodities. This fair-trade rose farm in Kenya grows up to 200,000 stems a day for the international market.

People power

Shoppers have people power. When they choose to buy fair-trade products rather than alternatives that have not been fairly traded, supermarkets see that there is a demand for more ethical goods. This means they are more likely to stock fair-trade products, which means better prices for more farmers and more likelihood that farmers will turn to fair trade.

Campaigning about things you disagree with is another way to show 'people power'. In 2017, the UK supermarket Sainsbury's sparked controversy by deciding to drop the internationally recognised 'Fairtrade' mark and replacing it with their own 'fairly traded' label, which campaigners say will take control away from producers. Over 100,000 people signed a petition asking the supermarket to reconsider.

What can you do?

Find out more about fair trade at www.fairtrade.org.uk and buy fairly traded goods wherever possible. Remember that every time you buy something that has the Fairtrade logo, you are supporting the person who produced it and the whole market for fairly traded goods.

Natural resources

The environment is closely linked to poverty. In many parts of the world, the poor depend most on natural resources for their livelihoods, so they are most affected by environmental issues such as climate change and deforestation. Tragically, countries that have the greatest natural wealth can still be the poorest on the planet.

Harming the environment

Caring for our planet and understanding the damage we are doing to it should concern every one of us. We are using up the Earth's resources faster than they can ever be replaced and so they will eventually run out. And there is another problem: burning fossil fuels (for example coal or oil) to make electricity and in vehicle engines is leading to global warming and climate change.

Population, pollution and poverty

In 1950, there were 2.5 billion people in the world. By 2100, there may be more than 11 billion. A bigger population means resources are used up more quickly and creates more pollution. But this is also unequal – the richest countries use up more resources, demand more goods and damage the environment far more than poorer countries – but the worst resource shortages are in the poorest countries. Another problem is that developing countries often want to industrialise in order to grow economically, but are unlikely to have the technology that means they can do this in a less-polluting way.

CASE STUDY

Wealth and poverty in DRC

Gold, diamonds, copper, uranium and oil are just some of the natural resources in the Democratic Republic of the Congo (DRC). The country also has a good climate, fertile soil and an abundant source of water from the world's second largest river. So, with an estimated wealth of US $24 trillion, DRC should be one of the richest countries on Earth. In fact, a remorseless history of slavery, colonialism, conflict and corruption means that it is one of the world's ten poorest.

This 12-year-old girl is just one of the 3.8 million internally displaced people who have been forced to leave their homes in DRC due to years of violent conflict.

Natural disasters and climate change

Poor people are also very vulnerable to natural disasters, such as flooding, earthquakes and tsunamis. Because climate change makes these kinds of extreme weather more probable, this problem is likely to increase in the future. Again, unfairly, richer countries such as the USA create far more of the carbon dioxide (a gas that fuels global warming) than the countries that struggle to cope with the effects of extreme weather.

China is the biggest emitter of carbon dioxide, followed by the USA. However, the USA's per capita emissions are more than double China's – this is because the USA's population is less than a quarter of the size of China's.

Honduras is one of the world's poorer countries. It is also the most likely to suffer from extreme weather such as hurricanes.

What can you do?

Global pollution fuels climate change and leads to natural disasters that devastate poor communities. Find out the size of your 'ecological footprint' (the impact you make on the planet) and how to reduce it at wwf.panda.org/how_you_can_help/live_green/.

Overpopulation

So the world's population is rising dramatically and this has an impact on the environment and therefore on poverty. But does overpopulation cause poverty? Family sizes are highest in poorest countries and it is the poorest people in those countries who have the largest families – so are people poor because they have too many children?

Rapid population growth is actually thought to be a symptom, not a cause, of poverty. In some societies, people want to have many children because in rural areas, for example, they help out with farming, at home or by looking after younger children. Another reason may be so that the parents have someone to look after them in old age. In the past, many children died from illness or hunger and this may be why some parents felt the need to have many children.

Large families are also linked to health and education. Where women have more access to these services, fertility levels go down.

The poverty cycle

All around the world, children born into poor families are more likely to be poor when they grow up. Poor children are less likely to be healthy – they tend to eat less nutritious food and live in poorer quality housing, while a poorer neighbourhood may have fewer facilities and fewer job opportunities. However, of course not every child born into poverty will grow up to be poor – and education can be one route out of poverty.

Education

A good education (see also pages 34–35) and qualifications can lead to a well-paid job. Education can also address other issues related to poverty, such as giving people information about different aspects of health – so in many ways, it is a large part of the solution to poverty. But sadly not every child has the same opportunities when it comes to education. In wealthier countries, all children attend primary and secondary school and many go on to college or university. In poorer countries or areas, many children get little or no schooling. Schools may also have very large classes and limited resources, making it harder for children to learn.

Access to education has improved dramatically in Togo, which is one of the 12 poorest countries in the world. In 1990, only 64.5 per cent of children were enrolled in primary school; by 2015, this had risen to 95.4 per cent.

Safety nets

In richer countries, there are 'safety nets' designed to help the poorest in society – governments provide benefits for the sick and unemployed, while retired people receive pensions. In poorer countries, there are no safety nets such as these. Poor people find it hard to get a loan if they need to borrow money and are unlikely to own anything of much value they can sell. They can ask their family and friends for help, but they are likely to be in the same situation.

Perhaps one of the most shocking statistics relating to poverty is that half of the world's poor are children. People in poverty are also more likely to come from large families, live in rural areas and have low levels of education.

The poverty map

Although the total number of people in extreme poverty has gone down in recent years, this has not been even across regions and countries. Much of the progress has been in the East Asia and Pacific region, which in 1990 had been home to half the world's poor, but by 2013 had less than 10 per cent. Therefore, the overall global decline masks the fact that poverty is still a critical issue in sub-Saharan Africa, which now has just over half of the world's poor.

SHARE OF GLOBAL POOR
BY REGION (%)

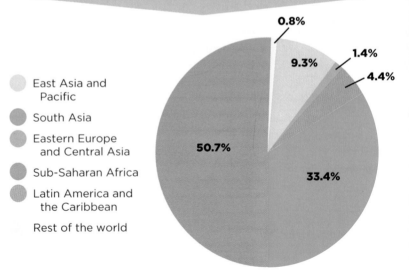

East Asia and
Pacific

South Asia

Eastern Europe
and Central Asia

Sub-Saharan Africa

Latin America and
the Caribbean

Rest of the world

0.8%
9.3%
1.4%
4.4%
50.7%
33.4%

This chart, which uses 2013 data, shows where the world's poor are living. There are more people in extreme poverty in sub-Saharan Africa than in all the other regions combined.

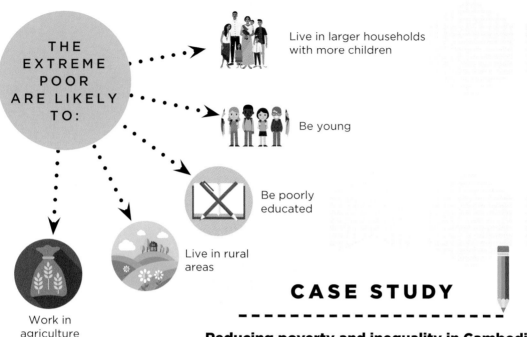

THE EXTREME POOR ARE LIKELY TO:

Live in larger households with more children

Be young

Be poorly educated

Live in rural areas

Work in agriculture

Urban vs rural

Poverty is far higher in rural areas than urban areas – in fact, a massive 80 per cent of the world's poor live in rural areas and 65 per cent work in agriculture (farming).

Garment (clothing) exports are 80 per cent of Cambodia's total exports. Research shows that the garment industry is benefiting the poorest people, as it mainly employs female migrants from rural areas.

CASE STUDY

Reducing poverty and inequality in Cambodia

Between 1970 and 1975, Cambodia, in Southeast Asia, was the scene of a vicious civil war. Then, from 1975 to 1979, it witnessed a horrific genocide in which approximately two million people – a quarter of the total population – died. This left the country facing huge challenges and many people in poverty, particularly in rural areas.

Now, Cambodia is one of the most rapidly growing economies in the world; the economy has grown by seven per cent or more every year since 2007. In the past, Cambodia's economy was based mostly on farming, but many people now work in the expanding clothing, tourism and service sectors. Great steps have been taken in terms of reducing inequality – many Cambodians, including the rural poor, have benefited from the country's economic growth.

Child poverty

Children account for nearly half the world's poor. Poverty particularly affects babies and children because they rely on others to provide for them and they are more vulnerable to disease, hunger and excessive heat or cold. Child poverty is not only a problem in the developing world – one in four children are living in poverty in the world's richest countries.

In 2017, it was reported that child poverty in the UK was up by four million. A staggering 67 per cent (two-thirds) of these children come from working families.

Child mortality

In the past, more babies and young children died than they do now, as a result of illnesses, living in unhealthy conditions or hunger. Between 1990 and 2015, the worldwide under-five mortality (death) rate went down by 53 per cent. This means that in 2015, 19,000 fewer children were dying *each day* than in 1990. However, there is still a massive gap between rich and poor. The rate of child mortality is about 11 times worse in poorer countries, and it is particularly high in Africa. Tragically, the number exceeds 100 deaths for every 1,000 births – or one in ten – in a number of countries, including Somalia, Chad, Central African Republic and Sierra Leone.

In high-income countries in 2016, the average rate of deaths per 1,000 live births was

5

In low-income countries in 2016, it was

73

deaths per 1,000 live births.

Child labour

Although children take part in paid and unpaid work all around the world, they are considered to be child labourers if they are too young to work, or when what they are doing may affect their health or development. For example, over 100 million children around the world work in sectors such as agriculture and mining, where they are exposed to danger and toxic chemicals. According to the children's charity Unicef, around one in four children (age 5–14) in the least developed countries is involved in child labour.

In most places, girls are just as likely as boys to be child labourers. This Nepalese girl is working in a brick factory.

Girls and women

If you include paid and unpaid work (such as looking after children and household tasks), women work longer hours than men. However, across the world and across all sectors, women earn less than men. In fact, women in full-time work on average earn 70–90 per cent of what men earn. Lone mothers with children are more likely to be poor than lone fathers with children. Among older people (65+) who live alone, women are more likely to be poor than men.

What can you do?

Many poverty charities focus on girls and women because of the discrimination they face, and because educating women can improve child mortality and help to raise a whole family out of poverty. Find out more at www.careinternational.org.uk/fighting-poverty and plan-uk.org/act-for-girls/about-because-i-am-a-girl.

All people have basic human rights, such as the right to an education and the right to keep themselves and their families fed, housed and healthy. But these basic rights are often out of reach for the people who need them the most – those in extreme poverty.

Going hungry

According to the United Nations (UN), 795 million people go hungry every day – that's one in every nine people. You might think that means we need to produce more food, but in fact the world already produces enough food to feed everyone. The reasons so many people go hungry are poverty and waste.

Food poverty

How much food a person can buy depends both on how much they earn and the price of food. People in poorer countries spend far more of their income on food than those in richer countries. Also, in recent years, food prices have gone up, but farmers have been paid less.

Waste and loss

Unbelievably, around a third of the food produced is lost or wasted. Loss refers to food that is spoiled or spilled before it is sold, for example, during harvesting, storing, packing or transportation. Waste is any food that is not consumed after this point – for example food thrown out by supermarkets or consumers.

Each year, around 222 million tonnes of food in richer countries is wasted – that's almost as much as the total amount of food produced in sub-Saharan Africa (230 million tonnes).

Famine

A famine is an extreme scarcity of food. There are multiple reasons why a famine may occur, including poverty, conflict, crop failure, climate change and government policies. There have been famines throughout history in all parts of the world, but in the twenty-first century, famines have been most widespread in Africa. Shockingly, although the number of deaths due to famine has dropped dramatically over the last few decades, famine is still an urgent issue.

A mother weighs her malnourished child in South Sudan in May 2017.

CASE STUDY

Famines in Yemen, South Sudan, Somalia and northeastern Nigeria

In 2017, the UN reported the biggest humanitarian crisis since the organisation began in 1945. More than 20 million people in these four countries face famine and starvation. Conflict is the major cause: there has been civil war in Somalia since 1991, in South Sudan since 2013 and in Yemen since 2015. In northeastern Nigeria, an uprising by the Islamic extremist group Boko Haram has forced 2.6 million people to flee their homes.

The double burden of malnutrition

People suffering food poverty does not just mean the victims of terrible famines. Many millions of people do not starve to death, but they do not get enough of the right kinds of nourishing food to thrive. Conversely, in many developed countries, there is a link between poverty and obesity. Being either underweight or obese are among the top ten risk factors for disease – the World Health Organization calls this the 'double burden of malnutrition'.

The OECD predicts that by 2030, obesity levels will be particularly high in the USA (47 per cent), Mexico (39 per cent) and England (35 per cent).

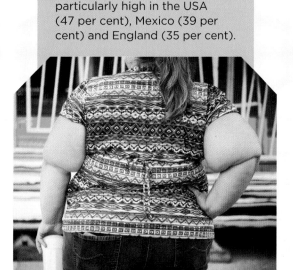

Housing and shelter

What does the word 'home' mean to you? Perhaps it makes you think about your family or the people who live with you, or maybe what your house looks like or where it is. It's unlikely that what you think of includes no toilet, no water or no electricity – but this is the reality for millions of people around the world.

These shanties are in the Dharavi area of Mumbai, India's largest slum.

Slums and shanty towns

A slum is a run-down, overcrowded part of a city. A shanty town is an area, usually on the outskirts of a city, made up of roughly built homes known as shacks or shanties. Hundreds of millions of people live in slums or shanty towns around the world. They often lack services such as electricity, clean water and law enforcement.

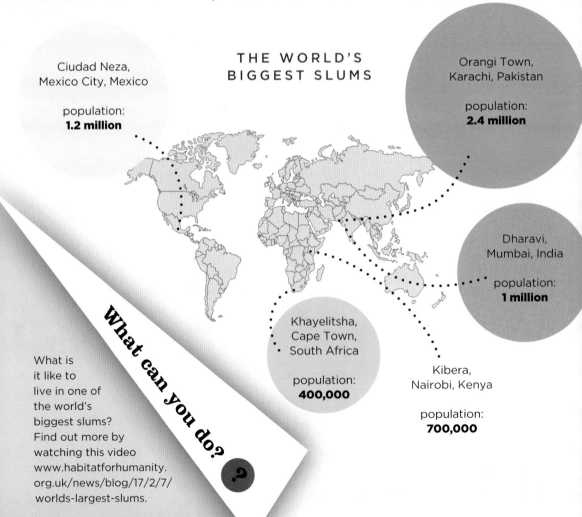

THE WORLD'S BIGGEST SLUMS

Ciudad Neza, Mexico City, Mexico

population:
1.2 million

Orangi Town, Karachi, Pakistan

population:
2.4 million

Dharavi, Mumbai, India

population:
1 million

Khayelitsha, Cape Town, South Africa

population:
400,000

Kibera, Nairobi, Kenya

population:
700,000

What can you do?

What is it like to live in one of the world's biggest slums? Find out more by watching this video www.habitatforhumanity. org.uk/news/blog/17/2/7/ worlds-largest-slums.

Homelessness

Although it is hard to get accurate data for homelessness, it is thought that around 100 million people around the world are homeless and 1.6 billion do not have adequate housing. You have probably seen homeless people sleeping on the streets of your town or city, but the reality is that many more families or individuals are homeless but not sleeping rough. They may be in temporary accommodation such as hostels or refuges, or staying temporarily on the floors of friends or relatives.

Lack of shelter is not just a problem in poorer countries, but right across the world – this woman is one of approximately 500,000 homeless people in the USA.

People become homeless for a complex variety of reasons – some may be personal (such as debts, alcohol or drug abuse, family breakdown, including domestic violence, or poor physical or mental health), while others may be to do with unemployment or housing policies. In developed countries, homelessness makes it hard for people to access education or get jobs, which means they can become trapped in poverty.

'Home' can mean different things to different people, but we all have the right to adequate housing and shelter.

27

Life expectancy

One of simplest ways to measure poverty is life expectancy – how many years people are expected to live for. Tragically, but not surprisingly, there is a strong link between poverty and low life expectancy. For example, in 2015: in Singapore, one of the richest countries in the world, life expectancy at birth was 83.1; in Sierra Leone, one of the poorest, it was just 50.1. The good news is that life expectancy rose in all regions between 2000 and 2015.

LIFE EXPECTANCY

66.4

71.4

2000   **2015**

Average global life expectancy rose by five years between 2000 and 2015. The greatest rise (of nearly ten years) was in Africa, but life expectancy in the region is still more than ten years below the global average.

Healthcare

Medicine can be expensive, so if poor people get sick, they may have to treat themselves or go without medical help. If people can afford healthcare, there may be no facilities nearby or they may have minimal supplies and few trained staff. Tragically, poor children often die from diseases that are largely preventable. Although the situation is improving, almost half a million children under five died as a result of diarrhoea in 2015.

This picture shows children being treated for diarrhoea in a makeshift camp in Dhaka, Bangladesh, in 2017. The number of cases is rising due to hotter temperatures and a shortage of pure drinking water.

Poverty and health

However, it is important to realise that there are exceptions – a lack of wealth does not have to mean poor health and low life expectancy. Poorer countries can still manage their resources well and improve the lives of their people significantly as a result.

CASE STUDY

Healthcare in Cuba

Cuba is a relatively poor country, but in terms of healthcare it outperforms not just other low- and medium-income countries, but some high-income countries too. Spending on health per capita is US $2475 (11.1 per cent of GDP) compared with US $9403 (17.1 per cent of GDP) in the nearby USA, but life expectancy is very similar. Cuba has a high number of healthcare workers: just under eight doctors for every 1,000 people. Compare that with both the USA and UK, where the figure is less than three for every 1,000.

The Cuban system focuses on prevention rather than cure – every single Cuban has an annual health check-up, often in their own home. Doctors do not just check things like blood pressure, but also assess the person's home and job to see how these might be affecting their health.

The Cuban system of prevention reduces pressure on hospitals.

Water for life

Water is precious – we all need it for drinking, washing, cleaning and cooking. You might not think twice before turning on a tap for a drink of water, flushing the toilet or running a bath, but the fact is that the developed world uses too much water, and rising populations and climate change put even more of a strain on this vital resource. An incredible 663 million people around the world don't have access to clean water.

Health and hygiene

To be healthy, people need safe water and to practise good hygiene. Unclean water and unhygenic conditions are directly linked to fatal diseases such as cholera and diarrhoea. They are also linked to other health problems such as pneumonia and trachoma, an infection that is the world's leading cause of preventable blindness.

People living in the slums in Mumbai, India, do not have easy access to clean water. These children are using containers to collect their water from a well.

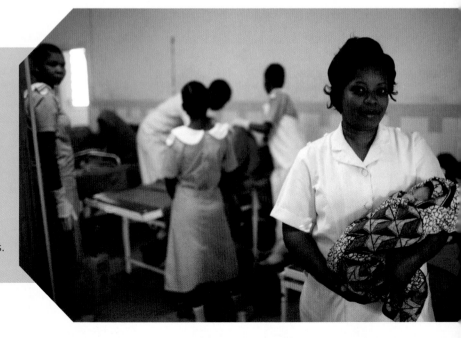

The healthcare workers in this Tanzanian hospital know the importance of clean water for staff and patients, but clean piped water only runs for one hour a day in the wards.

Collecting water

Many millions of people have to trek long distances to collect water – and it may not even be clean water. This job often falls to girls and women, which limits their opportunities for education and therefore their future lives. It also leaves them vulnerable to attack, especially in war zones.

These girls in Timor-Leste enjoy the new tap stand in their village provided by WaterAid. Before this, people in their community had to walk for two hours to collect water.

What can you do?

Wateraid is an international charity that aims to change the lives of the world's poorest people by improving access to safe water and sanitation. Read some amazing stories of how they help change lives at www.wateraid.org/uk/stories-from-our-work-around-the-world.

Sanitation

Closely linked to the importance of clean water is the importance of good sanitation (drainage and getting rid of sewage). Around the world, 2.4 billion people don't have access to adequate sanitation – that's one in every three. Many people are forced to go to the toilet in the open, which spreads deadly diseases.

Kibera in Nairobi, Kenya, is the largest slum in Africa. This picture shows people walking alongside an open sewer.

Girls and women

Girls and women are particularly at risk from harassment or attack if they are forced to go to the toilet in the open. Once girls start having periods, they may drop out of school if there are no private toilets.

What can you do?

Toilet Twinning is a fundraising initiative where you can donate money to 'twin' your toilet with one in an area of need. Find out how your school could be involved at www.toilettwinning.org/group/schools/.

These Ugandan girls are proud of the new toilet block at their school. 72 per cent of people in Uganda do not have access to safe, private toilets.

Waste

In many poorer countries, there is no system for disposing of waste. Rubbish is just left in piles near homes, where it can attract pests. If it is burned, it may release choking or toxic fumes. On a local scale, this can affect the health of people living nearby; on a wider, global scale, it contributes to the pollution of the whole planet.

Rubbish piles up near homes in this poor area of Myanmar.

Education

Education is a right for all people throughout life. It can change lives, and many people believe it is at the heart of ending poverty and making a more sustainable future. The infographic below, based on data from UNESCO, explains how education can improve many areas of life.

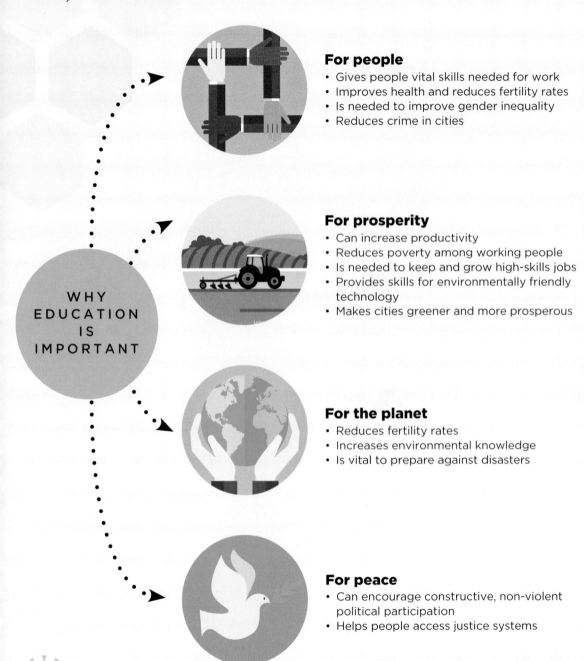

WHY EDUCATION IS IMPORTANT

For people
- Gives people vital skills needed for work
- Improves health and reduces fertility rates
- Is needed to improve gender inequality
- Reduces crime in cities

For prosperity
- Can increase productivity
- Reduces poverty among working people
- Is needed to keep and grow high-skills jobs
- Provides skills for environmentally friendly technology
- Makes cities greener and more prosperous

For the planet
- Reduces fertility rates
- Increases environmental knowledge
- Is vital to prepare against disasters

For peace
- Can encourage constructive, non-violent political participation
- Helps people access justice systems

Schooling

Enrolment in primary education in developing countries has improved substantially, but around 60 million children of primary-school age are still out of school and more than half of these are in sub-Saharan Africa. A major reason is conflict – half the children who are not in school live in conflict-afflicted areas. The cost of fees means some poor children never attend school and many more are lucky to complete primary school. For those who do attend, children in poorer areas are still often at a disadvantage – classes may be very big, the teacher may not have much training, and resources such as books may be limited.

Gender differences

The difference between the number of girls compared to the number of boys in school globally has been steadily improving – more than two-thirds of countries have what is called gender parity. This is a number that represents the ratio of girls to boys – for gender parity, you are looking for a GPI value of about one.

Both girls and boys attend this village school in Nepal. However, keeping girls in school in rural Nepal is still a challenge, as most drop out by the age of 12.

CASE STUDY

Girls' education in Nepal

Traditionally, girls have had very little education in rural Nepal. The reasons for this are poverty, an unsuitable school environment and cultural traditions – many people believe that girls do not need an education. In rural Nepal, parents start to look for a husband once their daughter reaches 14, and very few girls continue their education once they marry. Gender parity has improved greatly in Nepal over the last four decades – in 1975 the GPI was 0.186 – in 2015 it was 1.078.

What can you do?

ONE is an international organisation that campaigns to fight extreme poverty and disease. Its #GirlsCount campaign aims to make the world's longest video to persuade world leaders to get the 130 million girls without access to education into school. Find out how you can be part of it at www.one.org/us/take-action/poverty-is-sexist/.

GLOBAL GOALS

At the beginning of the twenty-first century, governments came together to agree eight goals that would make the world a better and fairer place. The goals had a specific timeframe – 15 years. In 2015, countries around the world announced new goals for the next 15 years.

Millennium Development Goals (MDGs)

In 2000, all the member states of the United Nations agreed to try and achieve eight development goals to meet the needs of the poorest people in the world.

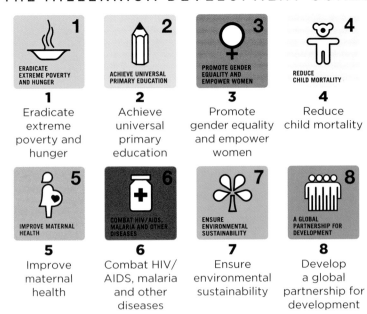

THE MILLENNIUM DEVELOPMENT GOALS

1 Eradicate extreme poverty and hunger

2 Achieve universal primary education

3 Promote gender equality and empower women

4 Reduce child mortality

5 Improve maternal health

6 Combat HIV/AIDS, malaria and other diseases

7 Ensure environmental sustainability

8 Develop a global partnership for development

Official logos of the Millennium Development Goals courtesy of UNDP Brazil

Each goal included specific targets to be achieved by 2015. For the first goal, these targets were:

1 Halve, between 1990 and 2015, the proportion of people whose income is less than US $1 a day*

2 Achieve full and productive employment and decent work for all, including women and young people

3 Halve, between 1990 and 2015, the proportion of people who suffer from hunger

The US $1 a day was raised to US $1.25 in 2008 and US $1.90 in 2015.

How successful were they?

In 2015, the UN reported that the goals had been largely successful across the globe, but acknowledged that there were still shortfalls. Also, although progress overall has been good, this has been uneven across regions and countries.

SUCCESSES

 1 Number of people living in extreme poverty fell from 1.9 billion (1990) to 836 million (2015)

 2 Huge improvements in gender equality in schooling

 3 More girls in school and more women in parliament

 4 Rate of children dying before their fifth birthday declined by more than half

 5 Maternal mortality ratio declined by 45 per cent worldwide

 6 Major improvements in fighting diseases such as HIV/AIDS, malaria and tuberculosis (TB)

 7 2.1 billion people have improved sanitation

SHORTFALLS

 1
- 800 million people still live in extreme poverty and suffer from hunger
- Poverty and hunger are particularly bad in countries affected by conflict

 3
- Gender inequality persists

 7
- Global emissions of carbon dioxide have increased over 50 per cent since 1990
- Water scarcity affects 40 per cent of people worldwide and is projected to increase

China achieved all of the MDGs by 2015 and made a large contribution to the global results. However, according to the country's own poverty standards, there were still 55 million poor people in rural areas in 2015.

Sustainable Development Goals (SDGs)

In 2015, the UN created 17 new goals to build on the MDGs – the Sustainable Development Goals. Each goal includes targets to be achieved by 2030.

THE SUSTAINABLE DEVELOPMENT GOALS

 1 End poverty in all its forms everywhere

 2 End hunger, achieve food security and improved nutrition and promote sustainable agriculture

 3 Ensure healthy lives and promote well-being for all at all ages

 4 Ensure inclusive and quality education for all and promote lifelong learning

 5 Achieve gender equality and empower all women and girls

 6 Ensure access to water and sanitation for all

 7 Ensure access to affordable, reliable, sustainable and modern energy for all

 8 Promote inclusive and sustainable economic growth, employment and decent work for all

 9 Build resilient infrastructure, promote sustainable industrialisation and foster innovation

 10 Reduce inequality within and among countries

 11 Make cities inclusive, safe, resilient and sustainable

 12 Ensure sustainable consumption and production patterns

 13 Take urgent action to combat climate change and its impacts

 14 Conserve and sustainably use the oceans, seas and marine resources

 15 Sustainably manage forests, combat desertification, halt and reverse land degradation, halt biodiversity loss

 16 Promote just, peaceful and inclusive societies

 17 Revitalise the global partnership for sustainable development

Official logos of the Sustainable Development Goals courtesy of the United Nations

Linked goals

Poverty is not a single issue, but one that is linked in to many other issues that are also addressed by the SDGs. In particular, it is closely tied to health, education, inequalities and issues around clean water and sanitation. It is also linked to the problems associated with climate change and the need for a more sustainable future.

Ending poverty and hunger

It is really positive that the number of people living in extreme poverty has more than halved since 1990, but 836 million people is still a huge number. The world is getting richer and it produces enough food for everyone, so no one should be going hungry in the twenty-first century. It is not surprising that the first two SDGs relate to ending poverty and hunger.

The UN says that there could be 150 million fewer hungry people in the world if women farmers had the same access to resources as men.

Goal 3 is to 'ensure healthy lives and promote well-being for all at all ages'.

Health and well-being

The third SDG relates to health. Although progress has been made in reducing diseases such as malaria, polio and the spread of HIV/AIDS, and reducing levels of child and maternal deaths, there are still many challenges. Every year, six million children still die before their fifth birthday and the maternal mortality ratio is still 14 times higher in developing regions than it is in developed regions. Health is also closely linked to the sixth SDG – to ensure access to water and sanitation for all.

Education and equality

Enrolment in primary school reached 91 per cent following the MDGs. However, 263 million children and young people (aged 6–17) are still out of school around the world. Most of these are girls and the gender gap widens as poverty increases.

Goals 4 and 5 relate to education for all and gender equality.

AGAINST POVERTY

Action

Many people care deeply about poverty all around the world. So what is being done to tackle it – and what can you do?

What is aid?

Aid is money mainly given by wealthier countries to help poorer countries; most of it comes from governments, while some comes from charities such as Oxfam. Aid can be divided into humanitarian aid and development aid.

Humanitarian aid

Humanitarian aid is given to help in emergency situations and aims to provide short-term relief. For example, in the UK, the Disasters Emergency Committee (DEC) is an umbrella organisation that is made up of a number of charities. It runs public appeals for money following crisis situations caused by wars, famines, earthquakes, floods and diseases, such as Ebola.

Following a devastating earthquake and tsunami in 2004, millions of people in countries including Sri Lanka lost their homes and livelihoods. The British public raised a vast £392 million in response to a DEC appeal.

Development aid

Development aid is money that is spent on longer-term projects to alleviate poverty, such as building schools and clean water systems. For example, the charity Practical Action (practicalaction.org) focuses on using technology to meet the twin challenges of poverty and climate change.

Loans and microcredit

Starting a successful business is one way for people to escape poverty, but starting a business costs money and banks will often not lend to the very poor. If the poorest people are able to borrow money, then the interest charged (how much it will cost them to pay the money back) may be very high, which can lead to even more serious problems. One alternative to this is microcredit, which means lending very small amounts of money at low interest rates to poorer people who want to start their own businesses.

CASE STUDY

Grameen Bank, Bangladesh

In 1983, Muhammad Yunus set up a bank that provided small, long-term loans to poor rural women. The women used the loans to buy chickens or goats or set up small businesses. They spent their income on food, healthcare and their children's education. By the end of 2015, Grameen Bank had 8.81 million borrowers, 97 per cent of whom were women. In 2006, Muhammad Yunus and the Grameen Bank were awarded the Nobel Peace Prize.

Following the success of the Grameen Bank, microcredit has been adopted by many countries in the developing world. This woman from Benin has used her loan to run a grocery store.

What can you do?

Fundraise (for example at school) and donate money to a charity that works to fight extreme poverty. One starting point to find out more is the organisation The Life You Can Save, which recommends what it considers to be the world's most effective charities: www.thelifeyoucansave.org/Top-Charities.

Can we end poverty?

We know there is enough food produced to feed everyone and we have the technology, medical knowledge and understanding to ensure that all people have the same opportunities regarding education and healthcare. But poverty continues – what are the solutions?

What can governments do?

Some people think poverty is best solved by a 'top down' approach – this means that governments should do more to help the poorest countries. Most aid is already given by governments, but there are criticisms of this. For example, some argue that people become dependent on aid, which keeps them in poverty. Others say that rich countries give money to countries for political rather than humanitarian reasons, and that money given may be used by corrupt governments for themselves or to buy weapons.

What can communities do?

Some campaigners think a 'bottom up' approach is a better way forward – that tackling poverty should start with the poor communities themselves. It is true that this can be very successful, but global poverty is such a huge issue that governments and international organisations need to be involved for big changes to take place. Charities such as WaterAid work with local partners to reach those most in need and with governments to develop sustainable strategies.

This man, who has trouble walking, now has a washroom in his home. Formerly he had to go to the field and needed someone to accompany him. This is thanks to a project by WaterAid and a local partner in Pakistan, funded by the UK's Department for International Development (DFID).

What can you do?

It can be hard to believe that individuals can do anything about global problems such as poverty, but the world is made up of billions of individuals. If every person thinks they can do nothing, then nothing gets done. If every person does something – even if that's a small thing – it can add up to a huge amount.

Ethical shopping

The poorest farmers on the planet may live half a world away from you, but it's likely that you and your family use their products – such as tea, coffee and sugar – every single day. All these products and many others can be bought fair trade, so check for the 'Fairtrade' logo when shopping. Another way to shop more ethically is to buy locally from independent shops, which helps support your own community.

Look for the Fairtrade logo when buying products such as bananas.

Tackle climate change

We all need to find solutions to the problems that are caused by climate change, so try to reduce your own impact on the planet as much as possible. There are lots of ways to do this, from big things like using more renewable energy (such as solar panels or wind turbines) to small things, such as planting a seed that will one day grow into a tree.

Action against poverty

WAYS TO REDUCE YOUR IMPACT ON THE ENVIRONMENT

Use cars less (share lifts, use public transport, walk or cycle where possible)

Use alternative energy sources, such as from solar panels or wind turbines, or use a 'green' energy supplier

Use energy-saving lights

Turn heating and hot water down slightly

Buy energy-efficient appliances

Turn appliances off when you're not using them

Plant a tree

Buy local produce or grow your own if possible

Think about what you buy – buy things with less packaging and reuse bags

Recycle as much as possible

Be aware

It may sound obvious, but one of the first steps in helping to tackle any big problem is to be aware of it. It can be hard to think about upsetting problems such as extreme poverty or hunger, and it is easy to feel overwhelmed – how can one person make a difference? But together, people can make their voices heard and start to take action.

Raise awareness

Start by finding out more about poverty – locally, nationally and across the world – and what we can do to tackle it. Then tell other people about it – this might mean your friends and family, your school or your government. You can write to your local council, the person who represents you in government (such as an MP) or the government of your country to tell them about the issues that matter to you. You can also lend your voice to campaigns such as ONE's campaign to tell world leaders that all girls count (see page 35).

Raise funds and donate

Another thing you can do is to support anti-poverty charities. Give money or donate goods to a local charity shop. When you are older, you could volunteer or even end up working for a charity as your career. You could also regularly donate food to a local food bank, perhaps by just buying two of a particular item when you are in the supermarket and then putting one of them in the food-bank collection point as you leave.

One way to help fight poverty is to donate to and buy goods from a charity shop such as Oxfam.

Your school

What can your school do? Perhaps you could raise money to support a charity or specific poverty project. Can your school become a Fairtrade school (see schools.fairtrade.org.uk)? Speak to your headteacher or board of governors.

Another option might be partnering with a school in another part of the world. This can become a hugely rewarding relationship on both sides, as one school can help to raise money for something they know is needed in the other school, teachers can talk to and perhaps visit one another, and children can write to each other and learn more about each other's countries.

Together for a fairer world

We all belong to the same world. We can all be more aware of global issues such as poverty, and we can all work together to try to tackle them to make a better and fairer future for everyone.

These Syrian refugee children may have had a life very different from yours, but they will have hopes and dreams about their future and the future of the world – just like you.

What can you do?

Oxfam produces lots of resources for children and young people. Find out more at www.oxfam.org.uk/ education.

GLOSSARY

carbon dioxide – a gas made when things are burned and which people and animals breathe out

climate change – the rising temperature of the Earth's surface and its effects, such as melting ice caps and more extreme weather

compensate – make up for

controversy – a big argument or disagreement

corruption – when people in power behave in a dishonest or immoral way

deforestation – chopping down trees or forests

DFID – Department for International Development, the UK government department responsible for overseas aid

emit – send out or release something, such as gas, into the atmosphere

extremist – describes very strong views or behaviours that most people do not agree with

famine – defined by the UN as when the death rate is more than two people per every 10,000 a day and there is more than 30 per cent acute malnutrition in children

fertility – the ability to have babies

fossil fuel – a natural fuel, such as coal or gas, formed from the remains of living organisms millions of years ago

GDP – gross domestic product, the total value of goods made and services provided in a country in one year

genocide – the attempt to destroy an ethnic, religious, national or racial group

global warming – the rising temperature of the Earth's surface

GPI – gender parity index, a way of measuring the relative access to education for girls and boys

humanitarian – to do with people's welfare and the reduction of suffering

industrialised – used to describe a country that has many industries (where things are produced in factories)

infrastructure – basic services a country needs, such as roads, buildings and power supplies

malnutrition – bad health caused by not having enough food or enough of the right kinds of food

maternal mortality ratio – a way of measuring the risks associated with pregnancy and childbirth

migrants – people that move from one area to another

nutritious – good for you

OECD – Organisation for Economic Co-operation and Development

per capita – average per person

persecution – when someone is treated badly because of their beliefs

pollution – damage caused to the natural world by harmful or poisonous substances

purchasing power – the value or amount of goods and services that can be bought with a unit of currency

rural – to do with the countryside

sustainable – not using resources that cannot be replaced or damaging the environment

tsunami – a long, high, sea wave, often caused by an earthquake

United Nations (UN) – an international organisation that works together to improve human rights and reduce wars

urban – to do with cities

FURTHER INFORMATION

Books

Loos Save Lives: How sanitation and clean water help prevent poverty, disease and death
Seren Boyd (Wayland, 2017)

Poverty and Hunger (Mapping Global Issues)
Cath Senker (Franklin Watts, 2011)

Ending Poverty and Hunger (Working for Our Future)
Judith Henegan (Franklin Watts, 2007)

Websites

Find out more about poverty on these websites:

www.globalgoals.org
Information about the Sustainable Development Goals

www.un.org/sustainabledevelopment/takeaction/
A list of things we can all do to work towards the SDGs

www.children.org/global-poverty/global-poverty-facts
Facts and issues about global poverty from the US charity Children International

INDEX

OUR WORLD IN CRISIS

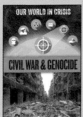     

9781445163710   9781445163734   9781445163772   9781445163758   9781445163819   9781445163796

Civil War and Genocide
978 1 4451 6371 0

Modern civil wars
War begins
Warfare
Life in a warzone
Fleeing from war
Human rights
Genocide
After a war
Moving on

Global Pollution
978 1 4451 6373 4

What is pollution?
The past
Air pollution
Soil pollution
Water pollution
Our changing climate
People and pollution
The future

Health and Disease
978 1 4451 6377 2

What are health and
 disease?
A healthy lifestyle
A healthy environment
Diseases
Fighting diseases
How diseases spread
Healthcare industries
Improving world health
The future

Immigration
978 1 4451 6375 8

What is immigration?
The past
The facts
Forced to flee
A better life
The impact of immigration
Arguing about
 immigration
The future

Poverty
978 1 4451 6381 9

What is poverty?
Why are people poor?
Who is poor?
Rights for life
Global goals
Action against
 poverty

Terrorism
978 1 4451 6379 6

What is terrorism?
History of terrorism
Religious terrorism
Political terrorism
Facts about terrorism
Fighting terrorism
Does terrorism work?
Responses to terrorism

W
FRANKLIN WATTS
LONDON•SYDNEY